MAD LIBS®

MAD MAD MAD MAD MAD LIBS

By Roger Price and Leonard Stern

PSS!
STERN SLOAN

ISBN 0-8431-7441-2

2004 Printing

PSS! and *MAD LIBS* are registered trademarks of Penguin Putnam Inc.

MAD⊙LIBS®
INSTRUCTIONS

MAD LIBS® is a game for people who don't like games!
It can be played by one, two, three, four, or forty.

• RIDICULOUSLY SIMPLE DIRECTIONS

In this tablet you will find stories containing blank spaces where words are
left out. One player, the READER, selects one of these stories. The READER
does not tell anyone what the story is about. Instead, he/she asks the other
players, the WRITERS, to give him/her words. These words are used to fill
in the blank spaces in the story.

• TO PLAY

The READER asks each WRITER in turn to call out a word—an adjective or
a noun or whatever the space calls for—and uses them to fill in the blank
spaces in the story. The result is a MAD LIBS® game.

When the READER then reads the completed MAD LIBS® game to the other
players, they will discover that they have written a story that is fantastic,
screamingly funny, shocking, silly, crazy, or just plain dumb—depending
upon which words each WRITER called out.

• EXAMPLE (*Before* and *After*)

" _____ !" he said _____
         EXCLAMATION   ADVERB

as he jumped into his convertible _____ and
                                              NOUN

drove off with his _____ wife.
                              ADJECTIVE

" *Ouch!* _____ !" he said *stupidly* _____
         EXCLAMATION   ADVERB

as he jumped into his convertible *cat* _____ and
                                              NOUN

drove off with his *brave* _____ wife.
                              ADJECTIVE

MAD LIBS®
QUICK REVIEW

In case you have forgotten what adjectives, adverbs, nouns, and verbs are, here is a quick review:

An ADJECTIVE describes something or somebody. *Lumpy, soft, ugly, messy,* and *short* are adjectives.

An ADVERB tells how something is done. It modifies a verb and usually ends in "ly." *Modestly, stupidly, greedily,* and *carefully* are adverbs.

A NOUN is the name of a person, place or thing. *Sidewalk, umbrella, bridle, bathtub,* and *nose* are nouns.

A VERB is an action word. *Run, pitch, jump,* and *swim* are verbs. Put the verbs in past tense if the directions say PAST TENSE. *Ran, pitched, jumped,* and *swam* are verbs in the past tense.

When we ask for a PLACE, we mean any sort of place: a country or city *(Spain, Cleveland)* or a room *(bathroom, kitchen.)*

An EXCLAMATION or SILLY WORD is any sort of funny sound, gasp, grunt, or outcry, like *Wow!, Ouch!, Whomp!, Ick!,* and *Gadzooks!*

When we ask for specific words, like a NUMBER, a COLOR, an ANIMAL, or a PART OF THE BODY, we mean a word that is one of those things, like *seven, blue, horse,* or *head.*

When we ask for a PLURAL, it means more than one. For example, *cat* pluralized is *cats.*

MAD LIBS® is fun to play with friends, but you can also play it by yourself! To begin with, DO NOT look at the story on the page below. Fill in the blanks on this page with the words called for. Then, using the words you have selected, fill in the blank spaces in the story.

Now you've created your own hilarious MAD LIBS® game!

NURSERY RHYMES

ADJECTIVE_____

ADVERB_____

PART OF THE BODY (PLURAL) _____

PART OF THE BODY (PLURAL) _____

ADJECTIVE_____

NOUN _____

VERB _____

TYPE OF LIQUID _____

NOUN _____

VERB ENDING IN "ING" _____

NOUN _____

ADJECTIVE_____

ADJECTIVE_____

PLURAL NOUN _____

PLURAL NOUN _____

NOUN _____

VERB (PAST TENSE)_____

PART OF THE BODY (PLURAL) _____

ADJECTIVE_____

VERB _____

NOUN _____

ADJECTIVE_____

MAD⊛LIBS®
NURSERY RHYMES

When some _____ school students were asked what
                    ADJECTIVE

nursery rhymes popped _____ into their _____
                            ADVERB   PART OF BODY (PLURAL)

or were on the tip of their _____, these were
                              PART OF BODY (PLURAL)

their _____ answers:
          ADJECTIVE

1. Jack and Jill went up the _____ to _____ a pail
                                NOUN   VERB

   of _____. Jack fell down and broke his _____
        TYPE OF LIQUID   NOUN

   and Jill came _____ after.
                  VERB ENDING IN "ING"

2. Mary, Mary, quite contrary, how does your _____
                                                    NOUN

   grow? With _____ bells and _____ shells and
                ADJECTIVE   ADJECTIVE

   _____ all in a row.
      PLURAL NOUN

3. Three blind _____, see how they run. They all went
                  PLURAL NOUN

   after the _____'s wife, who _____ off their
              NOUN   VERB (PAST TENSE)

   _____ with a/an _____ knife. Did you
      PART OF BODY (PLURAL)   ADJECTIVE

   ever _____ such a/an _____ in your life as
          VERB   NOUN

   three _____ mice?
            ADJECTIVE

MAD LIBS® is fun to play with friends, but you can also play it by yourself! To begin with, DO NOT look at the story on the page below. Fill in the blanks on this page with the words called for. Then, using the words you have selected, fill in the blank spaces in the story.

Now you've created your own hilarious MAD LIBS® game!

A VISIT TO THE DENTIST

PLURAL NOUN _____

PERSON IN ROOM (LAST NAME) _____

ADJECTIVE_____

NOUN _____

NOUN _____

PART OF THE BODY_____

PART OF THE BODY_____

PLURAL NOUN _____

NOUN _____

NOUN _____

EXCLAMATION_____

NOUN _____

NOUN _____

NOUN _____

VERB _____

NOUN _____

ADJECTIVE_____

NOUN _____

MAD LIBS®
A VISIT TO THE DENTIST

A one-act play to be performed by two _____ *in this room.*
PLURAL NOUN

PATIENT: Thank you so very much for seeing me, Doctor

_____ , on such _____ notice.
PERSON IN ROOM (LAST NAME)　　　　　ADJECTIVE

DENTIST: What is your problem, young _____ ?
NOUN

PATIENT: I have a pain in my upper _____ , which
NOUN

is giving me a severe _____ ache.
PART OF THE BODY

DENTIST: Let me take a look. Open your _____ wide.
PART OF THE BODY

Good. Now I'm going to tap your _____ with my _____ .
PLURAL NOUN　　　　　　NOUN

PATIENT: Shouldn't you give me a/an _____ killer?
NOUN

DENTIST: It's not necessary yet. _____ ! I think I see
EXCLAMATION

a/an _____ in your upper _____ .
NOUN　　　　　　　　　NOUN

PATIENT: Are you going to pull my _____ out?
NOUN

DENTIST: No. I'm going to _____ your tooth and put in
VERB

a temporary _____ .
NOUN

PATIENT: When do I come back for the _____ filling?
ADJECTIVE

DENTIST: A day after I cash your _____ .
NOUN

From MAD, MAD, MAD, MAD LIBS® • Copyright © 1998 by Price Stern Sloan,
a division of Penguin Putnam Books for Young Readers, New York.

MAD LIBS® is fun to play with friends, but you can also play it by yourself! To begin with, DO NOT look at the story on the page below. Fill in the blanks on this page with the words called for. Then, using the words you have selected, fill in the blank spaces in the story.

Now you've created your own hilarious MAD LIBS® game!

THE OSCARS

PLURAL NOUN _____

NOUN _____

NOUN _____

NOUN _____

ADJECTIVE_____

VERB _____

ADJECTIVE_____

PERSON IN ROOM _____

NOUN _____

PART OF BODY _____

ADJECTIVE_____

NOUN _____

ADJECTIVE_____

ADJECTIVE_____

ADJECTIVE_____

ADJECTIVE_____

NOUN _____

VERB ENDING IN "ING" _____

ADJECTIVE_____

PLURAL NOUN _____

MAD LIBS®
THE OSCARS

Thank you, ladies and _____. I'm so nervous.
PLURAL NOUN

My _____ is beating a/an _____ a minute.
NOUN   NOUN

I didn't prepare a/an _____. I never expected to win
NOUN

this _____ Oscar. I have so many people to
ADJECTIVE

_____. First and foremost, my _____
VERB   ADJECTIVE

co-star — _____ — who was always in my dressing
PERSON IN ROOM

_____, held my _____ when
NOUN   PART OF BODY

I was in trouble, and never failed to compliment me or give me a/an

_____ pat on my _____ when I did well.
ADJECTIVE   NOUN

I also want to thank my _____ director, my_____
ADJECTIVE   ADJECTIVE

producer, and of course, the _____ writer of the
ADJECTIVE

screenplay. Most of all, I want to thank you, my _____
ADJECTIVE

fans, and all the members of the Motion Picture _____
NOUN

who were responsible for my _____ this
VERB ENDING IN "ING"

_____ award. Bless your _____.
ADJECTIVE   PLURAL NOUN

From MAD, MAD, MAD, MAD LIBS® • Copyright © 1998 by Price Stern Sloan,
a division of Penguin Putnam Books for Young Readers, New York.

MAD LIBS® is fun to play with friends, but you can also play it by yourself! To begin with, DO NOT look at the story on the page below. Fill in the blanks on this page with the words called for. Then, using the words you have selected, fill in the blank spaces in the story.

Now you've created your own hilarious MAD LIBS® game!

BRINGING HOME THE GOOD ... OR IS IT BAD? ... NEWS

PERSON IN ROOM _____

ADJECTIVE _____

LETTER OF THE ALPHABET _____

LETTER OF THE ALPHABET _____

PLURAL NOUN _____

NOUN _____

NOUN _____

PART OF THE BODY _____

NOUN _____

ADJECTIVE _____

NOUN _____

NOUN _____

SAME PERSON IN ROOM _____

ADJECTIVE _____

ADJECTIVE _____

NOUN _____

ADVERB _____

PART OF THE BODY _____

NOUN _____

ADJECTIVE _____

ANOTHER PERSON IN ROOM (LAST NAME) _____

OCCUPATION_____

MAD LIBS®
BRINGING HOME THE GOOD
...OR IS IT BAD?...NEWS

Dear Parent,

Here is _____'s report card for the _____
       PERSON IN ROOM   ADJECTIVE

eighth grade. He/she has received a/an _____
                                     LETTER OF THE ALPHABET

in English, a/an _____ in Mathematics, and an
              LETTER OF THE ALPHABET

"A" in Social _____. Unfortunately, we could not
            PLURAL NOUN

give a passing _____ in _____ Education
            NOUN   NOUN

because his/her broken _____ prevented the taking of
                  PART OF THE BODY

the final _____. This _____ class can
        NOUN   ADJECTIVE

be made up in our summer _____. The school
                    NOUN

believes a "parent-_____ conference" is necessary to
             NOUN

discuss _____'s _____ behavior.
      SAME PERSON IN ROOM   ADJECTIVE

He/She continues to draw_____ pictures on the bathroom
               ADJECTIVE

_____ and talks _____ behind the teacher's
   NOUN   ADVERB

_____. Please call the principal's _____
PART OF THE BODY   NOUN

for a/an _____ appointment immediately.
      ADJECTIVE

                Sincerely,

                Ms. _____
                    ANOTHER PERSON IN ROOM (LAST NAME)

                Head _____
                      OCCUPATION

MAD LIBS® is fun to play with friends, but you can also play it by yourself! To begin with, DO NOT look at the story on the page below. Fill in the blanks on this page with the words called for. Then, using the words you have selected, fill in the blank spaces in the story.

Now you've created your own hilarious MAD LIBS® game!

CULTURAL STUFF

PLURAL NOUN _____

PLURAL NOUN _____

PART OF THE BODY (PLURAL) _____

ADJECTIVE_____

NOUN _____

VERB ENDING IN "ING" _____

ADJECTIVE_____

PERSON IN ROOM _____

PLURAL NOUN _____

NOUN _____

PLURAL NOUN _____

PLURAL NOUN _____

ADJECTIVE_____

ADJECTIVE_____

ADJECTIVE_____

PLURAL NOUN _____

ANOTHER PERSON IN ROOM _____

PLURAL NOUN _____

NOUN _____

MAD LIBS®
CULTURAL STUFF

I. BALLET

Ballet companies are springing up like _____ all
PLURAL NOUN

over the country. Ballet is a form of dance in which male and female

_____ tell a story through movement of their arms
PLURAL NOUN

and _____ to _____ music. Two of the best-
PART OF THE BODY (PLURAL)   ADJECTIVE

known ballets are _____ *Lake* and _____ *Beauty*.
NOUN   VERB ENDING IN "ING"

II. OPERA

Thanks to the three _____ tenors, Pavarotti, Domingo,
ADJECTIVE

and _____, opera is once again playing to packed
PERSON IN ROOM

_____ in every major _____ in the country.
PLURAL NOUN   NOUN

The sales of their tapes and compact _____ have established
PLURAL NOUN

this trio of tenors as America's favorite _____.
PLURAL NOUN

III. SYMPHONY

Classical music is making a/an _____ comeback these
ADJECTIVE

days. Symphony orchestras led by _____ conductors
ADJECTIVE

are once again playing the _____ melodies of such musical
ADJECTIVE

_____ as Bach, Beethoven and _____.
PLURAL NOUN   ANOTHER PERSON IN ROOM

Once again, auditoriums are filled with _____ of all ages,
PLURAL NOUN

who rejoice in listening to a violin solo or a _____ concerto.
NOUN

MAD LIBS® is fun to play with friends, but you can also play it by yourself! To begin with, DO NOT look at the story on the page below. Fill in the blanks on this page with the words called for. Then, using the words you have selected, fill in the blank spaces in the story.

Now you've created your own hilarious MAD LIBS® game!

INSTRUCTIONS FOR THE BABYSITTER

ADJECTIVE_____

PLURAL NOUN _____

PLURAL NOUN _____

PLURAL NOUN _____

PLURAL NOUN _____

NOUN _____

ADVERB_____

NOUN _____

TYPE OF LIQUID _____

VERB _____

NOUN _____

NOUN _____

ADJECTIVE_____

ADJECTIVE_____

NOUN _____

MAD LIBS®
INSTRUCTIONS FOR
THE BABAYSITTER

The boys can watch an hour of _____ television
ADJECTIVE

before turning off the _____ in their room. Make sure
PLURAL NOUN

they do not watch any violent _____ or adult _____.
PLURAL NOUN   PLURAL NOUN

If there are any phone _____, do not identify yourself as
PLURAL NOUN

the _____-sitter. Take a message. Write it _____
NOUN   ADVERB

on the _____ provided.
NOUN

Remember, the baby gets his warm _____ around six o'clock.
TYPE OF LIQUID

If the baby starts to _____ in his _____, be sure
VERB   NOUN

to change his diaper before you put him back in his _____.
NOUN

If you have any _____ questions or _____
ADJECTIVE   ADJECTIVE

problems, please page us on our _____.
NOUN

Good luck!

MAD LIBS® is fun to play with friends, but you can also play it by yourself! To begin with, DO NOT look at the story on the page below. Fill in the blanks on this page with the words called for. Then, using the words you have selected, fill in the blank spaces in the story.

Now you've created your own hilarious MAD LIBS® game!

ADVICE COLUMN

PERSON IN ROOM (FIRST NAME)_____

ADJECTIVE_____

NUMBER _____

NOUN _____

NOUN _____

PLURAL NOUN _____

VERB ENDING IN "ING" _____

NOUN _____

NUMBER _____

SAME PERSON IN ROOM (FIRST NAME) _____

NOUN _____

ADJECTIVE_____

NOUN _____

PLURAL NOUN _____

NOUN _____

ADVERB_____

NOUN _____

NOUN _____

NOUN _____

VERB _____

ADJECTIVE_____

NOUN _____

NOUN _____

MAD LIBS®
ADVICE COLUMN

Dear _____,
    PERSON IN ROOM (FIRST NAME)

My _____ daughter, who is only _____ years old,
        ADJECTIVE   NUMBER

wants to wear a mini _____ with a bare _____.
                          NOUN   NOUN

She claims all the other _____ her age are _____
                              PLURAL NOUN   VERB ENDING IN "ING"

them. What to do?

                    Signed,
                    An anxious _____
                                    NOUN

Dear "Anxious,"

Take my advice and ground your daughter for _____ days.
                                                    NUMBER

Dear _____,
    SAME PERSON IN ROOM (FIRST NAME)

My oldest _____ is a/an _____ slob. As
                NOUN   ADJECTIVE

often as I try, I can never get him to wash his _____, brush
                                                      NOUN

his _____, or comb his _____ before going to
        PLURAL NOUN   NOUN

school. He also _____ refuses to take a bath or a/an
                      ADVERB

_____, clean up his _____, or make up
        NOUN   NOUN

the very _____ he sleeps in. How can I _____?
              NOUN   VERB

                    Signed,
                    A/an _____ Mother
                              ADJECTIVE

Dear "Mother,"

You better clean that _____ up before he turns into a
                            NOUN

filthy ball of _____.
                    NOUN

MAD LIBS® is fun to play with friends, but you can also play it by yourself! To begin with, DO NOT look at the story on the page below. Fill in the blanks on this page with the words called for. Then, using the words you have selected, fill in the blank spaces in the story.

Now you've created your own hilarious MAD LIBS® game!

LOST AND FOUND

ADJECTIVE_____

NOUN _____

PART OF THE BODY (PLURAL) _____

ADJECTIVE_____

PERSON IN ROOM (FIRST NAME)_____

NOUN _____

ADVERB_____

NOUN _____

PLURAL NOUN _____

ADJECTIVE_____

TYPE OF VEGETABLE _____

NOUN _____

NOUN _____

ADJECTIVE_____

PART OF THE BODY _____

NOUN _____

ADJECTIVE_____

VERB ENDING IN "ING" _____

ADJECTIVE_____

NOUN _____

ADJECTIVE_____

NOUN _____

MAD LIBS®
LOST AND FOUND

LOST

Dog. A black and _____ Cocker _____ with
ADJECTIVE   NOUN

deep brown _____ and a very _____
PART OF THE BODY (PLURAL)   ADJECTIVE

tail. Answers to the name of _____.
PERSON IN ROOM (FIRST NAME)

LOST

A solid gold _____ with a/an _____
NOUN   ADVERB

carved wooden _____ hanging from it. Reward of
NOUN

50 _____ for the return of this _____ heirloom.
PLURAL NOUN   ADJECTIVE

LOST

Seven _____ diamond _____ with a sterling
TYPE OF VEGETABLE   NOUN

_____ clasp. Gift from _____ grandmother
NOUN   ADJECTIVE

Owner is _____ broken. Generous _____
PART OF THE BODY   NOUN

offered upon return.

FOUND

A/an _____ elephant in my _____ pool.
ADJECTIVE   VERB ENDING IN "ING"

He has _____ marks on his hide, a short _____,
ADJECTIVE   NOUN

and a very _____ trunk. Please come and get him.
ADJECTIVE

He's eating me out of house and _____!
NOUN

MAD LIBS® is fun to play with friends, but you can also play it by yourself! To begin with, DO NOT look at the story on the page below. Fill in the blanks on this page with the words called for. Then, using the words you have selected, fill in the blank spaces in the story.

Now you've created your own hilarious MAD LIBS® game!

POOL ROOLS

NOUN _____

ADJECTIVE _____

ADJECTIVE _____

VERB ENDING IN "ING" _____

ADJECTIVE _____

PLURAL NOUN _____

ADJECTIVE _____

PLURAL NOUN _____

NUMBER _____

NOUN _____

NOUN _____

VERB ENDING IN "ING" _____

ADJECTIVE _____

NOUN _____

ADJECTIVE _____

PLURAL NOUN _____

ADVERB _____

PART OF THE BODY _____

ADJECTIVE _____

NOUN _____

ADJECTIVE _____

MAD LIBS®
POOL ROOLS

ATTENTION ALL SWIMMERS!

If you want to swim in this _____ or soak in our
NOUN

_____ spa, you must follow these _____ rules.
ADJECTIVE   ADJECTIVE

1. No nude _____ allowed. Men must wear
VERB ENDING IN "ING"

_____ shorts, and women must wear one-piece
ADJECTIVE

bathing _____ or _____ bikinis.
PLURAL NOUN   ADJECTIVE

2. No _____ under the age of _____ are allowed in
PLURAL NOUN   NUMBER

the _____ unless accompanied by a/an _____ .
NOUN   NOUN

3. _____ in the pool is only permitted in the
VERB ENDING IN "ING"

_____ end and only when a life-_____
ADJECTIVE   NOUN

is on duty.

4. People with _____ hair must wear bathing _____ .
ADJECTIVE   PLURAL NOUN

WARNING! If you plan to sunbathe, _____ cover your
ADVERB

arms, legs, and _____ with a/an _____
PART OF THE BODY   ADJECTIVE

lotion. You don't want to get a/an _____ burn!
NOUN

Have a/an _____ day!
ADJECTIVE

MAD LIBS® is fun to play with friends, but you can also play it by yourself! To begin with, DO NOT look at the story on the page below. Fill in the blanks on this page with the words called for. Then, using the words you have selected, fill in the blank spaces in the story.

Now you've created your own hilarious MAD LIBS® game!

WHAT'S IN A NAME?

PLURAL NOUN _____

NOUN _____

NOUN _____

PART OF THE BODY _____

PLURAL NOUN _____

ADVERB _____

NOUN _____

ADJECTIVE _____

ADJECTIVE _____

NOUN _____

NOUN _____

PERSON IN ROOM (LAST NAME) _____

NOUN _____

NOUN _____

ADJECTIVE _____

MAD LIBS®
WHAT'S IN A NAME?

William Shakespeare is regarded by scholars and _____

_{PLURAL NOUN}

alike as the greatest playwright and _____ ever to put

_{NOUN}

pen to _____. Although he wrote in his native

_{NOUN}

_____, Shakespeare has been translated into twelve

_{PART OF THE BODY}

different _____ and his plays and poems are _____

_{PLURAL NOUN}   _{ADVERB}

read and performed everywhere in the world. Hamlet's soliloquy—

which begins "To be or not to be, that is the _____,"—

_{NOUN}

has been delivered on stage by more _____ actors

_{ADJECTIVE}

than any other _____ _____ ever written.

_{ADJECTIVE}   _{NOUN}

Among Shakespeare's greatest plays are *Hamlet*, *Romeo and Juliet*,

The _____ *of Venice*, *King* _____,

_{NOUN}   _{PERSON IN ROOM (LAST NAME)}

A Midsummer Night's _____, and *The Taming of*

_{NOUN}

the _____. We could go on, but we must leave. As Romeo

_{NOUN}

said to Juliet, "Parting is such _____ sorrow."

_{ADJECTIVE}

MAD LIBS® is fun to play with friends, but you can also play it by yourself! To begin with, DO NOT look at the story on the page below. Fill in the blanks on this page with the words called for. Then, using the words you have selected, fill in the blank spaces in the story.

Now you've created your own hilarious MAD LIBS® game!

A GOOD NIGHT'S SLEEP

ADJECTIVE _____

ADJECTIVE _____

PART OF THE BODY (PLURAL) _____

NOUN _____

ADVERB _____

ADVERB _____

PLURAL NOUN _____

ADJECTIVE _____

VERB _____

PLURAL NOUN _____

PART OF THE BODY _____

ADJECTIVE _____

TYPE OF LIQUID _____

NOUN _____

NOUN _____

ANIMAL (PLURAL) _____

NOUN _____

PART OF THE BODY _____

MAD LIBS®
A GOOD NIGHT'S SLEEP

Here are five _____ suggestions to follow if you want
ADJECTIVE

a/an _____ night's sleep:
ADJECTIVE

1. Open a window and fill your _____ with fresh
PART OF THE BODY (PLURAL)

_____ and then, exhale _____ .
NOUN   ADVERB

2. Exercise _____ at least 15 _____ a day.
ADVERB   PLURAL NOUN

Doctors and _____ therapists suggest a combination
ADJECTIVE

of push-ups and _____-ups, jumping _____ ,
VERB   PLURAL NOUN

and, of course, deep _____ bends.
PART OF THE BODY

3. Drink a/an _____ glass of warm _____
ADJECTIVE   TYPE OF LIQUID

a half hour before turning off your _____ and going to
NOUN

_____ .
NOUN

4. If all else fails, count _____ jumping over a/an
ANIMAL (PLURAL)

_____ .
NOUN

5. WARNING: Never go to bed on a full _____ .
PART OF THE BODY

From MAD, MAD, MAD, MAD LIBS® • Copyright © 1998 by Price Stern Sloan,
a division of Penguin Putnam Books for Young Readers, New York.

MAD LIBS® is fun to play with friends, but you can also play it by yourself! To begin with, DO NOT look at the story on the page below. Fill in the blanks on this page with the words called for. Then, using the words you have selected, fill in the blank spaces in the story.

Now you've created your own hilarious MAD LIBS® game!

LOOK IT UP

ADJECTIVE_____

NOUN _____

NOUN _____

PLURAL NOUN _____

ADVERB_____

ADVERB_____

NOUN _____

NOUN _____

NOUN _____

NOUN _____

PLURAL NOUN _____

PLURAL NOUN _____

ADVERB_____

NOUN _____

NOUN _____

NOUN _____

NOUN _____

NOUN _____

NOUN _____

MAD LIBS®
LOOK IT UP

A/An _____ dictionary is the essential reference
     ADJECTIVE

_____ for home, school, or _____.
  NOUN   NOUN

A dictionary not only defines _____, but tells you how
                                      PLURAL NOUN

to spell words _____ and how to pronounce them
                   ADVERB

_____. Dictionaries are available in local _____
   ADVERB   NOUN

stores or, if necessary, you can order one with a/an _____ card
                                             NOUN

over the Internet. For the average _____, a medium-sized
                                        NOUN

dictionary is best. For researchers, an unabridged _____,
                                             NOUN

which has more than 200,000 _____ will be needed.
                                PLURAL NOUN

For those who can't remember the meaning of any _____,
                                               PLURAL NOUN

a pocket-sized dictionary works _____. These dictionaries
                                  ADVERB

are small enough to fit in a woman's _____, the pocket of a
                                      NOUN

man's _____, or a kid's back _____. As
        NOUN   NOUN

Henry Wadsworth Longefellow, the famous _____ wrote,
                                          NOUN

"I'd rather go without food in my _____ than go
                                      NOUN

without a dictionary on my _____ shelf."
                              NOUN

MAD LIBS® is fun to play with friends, but you can also play it by yourself! To begin with, DO NOT look at the story on the page below. Fill in the blanks on this page with the words called for. Then, using the words you have selected, fill in the blank spaces in the story.

Now you've created your own hilarious MAD LIBS® game!

COFFEEHOUSES

NOUN _____

NOUN _____

ADJECTIVE _____

ADJECTIVE _____

NOUN _____

ADJECTIVE _____

ADJECTIVE _____

NOUN _____

PLURAL NOUN _____

TYPE OF LIQUID _____

PLURAL NOUN _____

VERB _____

NOUN _____

PLURAL NOUN _____

ADJECTIVE _____

ANOTHER TYPE OF LIQUID _____

PLURAL NOUN _____

PART OF THE BODY _____

VERB _____

PLURAL NOUN _____

PLURAL NOUN _____

PART OF THE BODY _____

MAD LIBS®
COFFEEHOUSES

Coffeehouses are in! Gone are the local corner _____
                                                      NOUN

and the neighborhood ice-cream _____. It doesn't matter
                                      NOUN

if you live in a/an _____ city or a/an _____
                         ADJECTIVE   ADJECTIVE

town, there is bound to be a coffee _____ in your
                                              NOUN

_____ neighborhood. Coffeehouses have become the place
   ADJECTIVE

where _____ friends gather, sit, and chew the _____,
          ADJECTIVE   NOUN

remembering the good old _____ as they sip their steaming
                              PLURAL NOUN

cups of _____. Coffeehouses cater to busy business
         TYPE OF LIQUID

_____, who use them to _____ million
   PLURAL NOUN   VERB

_____ deals. Coffeehouses are also favorite spots for single
   NOUN

men and _____, who love to linger over their mugs of
           PLURAL NOUN

_____ _____ as they watch the attractive
  ADJECTIVE   ANOTHER TYPE OF LIQUID

_____ go by, hoping to catch his or her _____,
  PLURAL NOUN   PART OF THE BODY

and maybe even _____ a date. Most evenings, coffeehouses
                    VERB

are filled by young lovers drinking out of each others' _____
                                                            PLURAL NOUN

as they whisper sweet _____ in each other's _____.
                          PLURAL NOUN   PART OF THE BODY

From MAD, MAD, MAD, MAD LIBS® • Copyright © 1998 by Price Stern Sloan,
a division of Penguin Putnam Books for Young Readers, New York.

MAD LIBS® is fun to play with friends, but you can also play it by yourself! To begin with, DO NOT look at the story on the page below. Fill in the blanks on this page with the words called for. Then, using the words you have selected, fill in the blank spaces in the story.

Now you've created your own hilarious MAD LIBS® game!

IT'S ABOUT TIME

PLURAL NOUN _____

PLURAL NOUN _____

PLURAL NOUN _____

NUMBER _____

PLURAL NOUN _____

NOUN _____

NOUN _____

NOUN _____

NOUN _____

PART OF THE BODY _____

LETTER OF THE ALPHABET _____

PLURAL NOUN _____

PLURAL NOUN _____

PLURAL NOUN _____

PART OF THE BODY _____

PART OF THE BODY _____

NUMBER _____

ADJECTIVE _____

NOUN _____

Thousands of _____ ago, there were calendars that
　　　　　　　　PLURAL NOUN

enabled the ancient _____ to divide a year into twelve
　　　　　　　　　　　PLURAL NOUN

_____, each month into _____ weeks, and each
　　PLURAL NOUN　　　　　　　　　　NUMBER

week into seven _____. At first, people told time by a
　　　　　　　　　PLURAL NOUN

sun clock, sometimes known as the _____ dial. Ultimately,
　　　　　　　　　　　　　　　NOUN

they invented the great timekeeping devices of today, such as the

grandfather _____, the pocket _____, the alarm
　　　　　　NOUN　　　　　　　　　　　NOUN

_____, and, of course, the _____ watch.
　　NOUN　　　　　　　　　　　　　PART OF BODY

Children learn about clocks and time almost before they learn their

AB _____'s. They are taught that a day consists of 24
　　LETTER OF THE ALPHABET

_____, an hour has 60 _____, and a minute has 60
　PLURAL NOUN　　　　　　　　　PLURAL NOUN

_____. By the time they are in kindergarten, they know if
　PLURAL NOUN

the big _____ is at twelve and the little _____
　　PART OF THE BODY　　　　　　　　　　PART OF THE BODY

is at three, that it is _____ o'clock. I wish we could continue this
　　　　　　　　　NUMBER

_____ lesson, but we've run out of _____.
　ADJECTIVE　　　　　　　　　　　　　　　NOUN

MAD LIBS® is fun to play with friends, but you can also play it by yourself! To begin with, DO NOT look at the story on the page below. Fill in the blanks on this page with the words called for. Then, using the words you have selected, fill in the blank spaces in the story.

Now you've created your own hilarious MAD LIBS® game!

LETTERS PARENTS HOPE GET LOST IN THE MAIL

ADVERB_____

NOUN _____

NOUN _____

ADJECTIVE_____

COLOR_____

NOUN _____

PART OF THE BODY _____

PERSON IN ROOM (MALE)_____

NOUN _____

ADJECTIVE_____

PERSON IN ROOM (FEMALE)_____

ADVERB_____

NOUN _____

PLURAL NOUN _____

ADJECTIVE_____

NOUN _____

PART OF THE BODY _____

NUMBER _____

NOUN _____

ADJECTIVE_____

ANOTHER PERSON IN ROOM (MALE)_____

ANIMAL _____

PART OF THE BODY _____

PART OF THE BODY _____

VERB _____

SAME ANIMAL _____

MAD LIBS®
LETTERS PARENTS HOPE
GET LOST IN THE MAIL

Dear Folks,

I'm in L.A. It is _____ awesome. Yesterday, I met the greatest
                     ADVERB

_____ . He plays _____ with a/an _____
        NOUN   NOUN   ADJECTIVE

band. He has _____ hair and wears a/an _____
                    COLOR   NOUN

in his _____ . I can't wait for you to meet
              PART OF BODY

_____ , the _____ of my dreams.
  PERSON IN ROOM (MALE)   NOUN

            Your _____ daughter,
                      ADJECTIVE

            _____
              PERSON IN ROOM (FEMALE)

Dear Folks,

Please send money as _____ as possible. I found a really great
                           ADVERB

surf _____ for only 150 _____ . I borrowed the money from
       NOUN   PLURAL NOUN

my _____ girlfriend, who is a life _____ at the beach and is
      ADJECTIVE   NOUN

teaching me to surf nine-_____ waves. Although she is
                            PART OF THE BODY

_____ years older than I am, I know she's the right _____ for me.
 NUMBER   NOUN

            Your _____ son,
                      ADJECTIVE

            _____
              PERSON IN ROOM (MALE)
            (known to my beach friends as The _____)
                                                   ANIMAL

Dear Folks,

For your information, I broke my _____ surfing, so I
                                    PART OF THE BODY

returned the surfboard. P.S. I used the money to get a tattoo on my

_____ . You'll _____ it!
  PART OF THE BODY   VERB

            Signed, The _____
                           SAME ANIMAL

From MAD, MAD, MAD, MAD LIBS® • Copyright © 1998 by Price Stern Sloan,
a division of Penguin Putnam Books for Young Readers, New York.

MAD LIBS® is fun to play with friends, but you can also play it by yourself! To begin with, DO NOT look at the story on the page below. Fill in the blanks on this page with the words called for. Then, using the words you have selected, fill in the blank spaces in the story.

Now you've created your own hilarious MAD LIBS® game!

A CONCERT REVIEW

NOUN _____

FOOD _____

PLURAL NOUN _____

PLURAL NOUN _____

PLURAL NOUN _____

ADJECTIVE _____

NONSENSE WORD _____

ADJECTIVE _____

NOUN _____

PLURAL NOUN _____

PART OF THE BODY (PLURAL) _____

PERSON IN ROOM _____

ANIMAL _____

PLURAL NOUN _____

PART OF THE BODY _____

PLURAL NOUN _____

ADVERB _____

PLURAL NOUN _____

NOUN _____

MAD LIBS®
A CONCERT REVIEW

Throughout last night's _____, the cheering for the
NOUN

performance of Pearl _____ was so deafening, you had to
FOOD

hold your _____ over your _____. Many well-
PLURAL NOUN   PLURAL NOUN

known _____ are calling it the _____ concert
PLURAL NOUN   ADJECTIVE

of the decade. For their opening number, the band played their hit

song, "_____," followed by their _____ rendition
NONSENSE WORD   ADJECTIVE

of "I Can't Get No _____." Then, as a tribute to the Beatles,
NOUN

they played several _____ from the hit album, *Sergeant*
PLURAL NOUN

Pepper's Lonely _____ *Club Band*. Unfortunately,
PART OF THE BODY (PLURAL)

throughout the performance, lead singer _____
PERSON IN ROOM

moved about the stage like a caged _____, singing at the top
ANIMAL

of his/her _____, giving this critic a terrible _____
PLURAL NOUN   PART OF THE BODY

ache. However, the concert ended with the audience standing on

their _____ and applauding _____, forcing
PLURAL NOUN   ADVERB

the group to come back for three _____ before the
PLURAL NOUN

_____ finally came down.
NOUN

MAD LIBS® is fun to play with friends, but you can also play it by yourself! To begin with, DO NOT look at the story on the page below. Fill in the blanks on this page with the words called for. Then, using the words you have selected, fill in the blank spaces in the story.

Now you've created your own hilarious MAD LIBS® game!

NEXT-DOOR NEIGHBORS

PLURAL NOUN _____

NOUN _____

ADJECTIVE _____

NOUN _____

NOUN _____

NOUN _____

ADJECTIVE _____

NOUN _____

ADJECTIVE _____

TYPE OF FOOD _____

ADVERB _____

NOUN _____

NOUN _____

PLURAL NOUN _____

ADJECTIVE _____

NOUN _____

NOUN _____

PLURAL NOUN _____

ADJECTIVE _____

PLURAL NOUN _____

MAD☻LIBS®
NEXT-DOOR NEIGHBORS

We have new _____ living in the _____ next
            PLURAL NOUN   NOUN

door. He is a/an _____ salesman for a/an _____
                   ADJECTIVE   NOUN

company, and she teaches _____ in a private _____.
                            NOUN   NOUN

Last night, we were invited to their _____ home for a
                                          ADJECTIVE

potluck _____. We brought a/an _____ _____
           NOUN   ADJECTIVE   TYPE OF FOOD

casserole. After dinner, we went into their _____ decorated
                                              ADVERB

family _____, sat in front of their roaring _____, and
          NOUN   NOUN

toasted _____. Before we left, our host insisted on taking
          PLURAL NOUN

out his _____ _____ — which we mistook for
          ADJECTIVE   NOUN

an ancient _____ — to play a few country _____
              NOUN   PLURAL NOUN

on it. All in all, it was an _____ evening, and since then,
                              ADJECTIVE

the four of us have become as thick as _____.
                                           PLURAL NOUN

MAD LIBS® is fun to play with friends, but you can also play it by yourself! To begin with, DO NOT look at the story on the page below. Fill in the blanks on this page with the words called for. Then, using the words you have selected, fill in the blank spaces in the story.

Now you've created your own hilarious MAD LIBS® game!

CELLULAR PHONES

NUMBER _____

PLURAL NOUN _____

ADJECTIVE _____

VERB ENDING IN "ING" _____

NOUN _____

ADVERB _____

PART OF THE BODY _____

PLURAL NOUN _____

PLURAL NOUN _____

ADVERB _____

ADJECTIVE _____

NOUN _____

NUMBER _____

PLURAL NOUN _____

NOUN _____

VERB ENDING IN "ING" _____

NOUN _____

NOUN _____

NUMBER _____

ADJECTIVE _____

PLURAL NOUN _____

PART OF THE BODY _____

MAD LIBS®
CELLULAR PHONES

A recent survey informs us that one out of every _____

NUMBER

_____ owns a/an _____ phone. Fortunately,

PLURAL NOUN   ADJECTIVE

_____ over a mobile _____ in recent years

VERB ENDING IN "ING"   NOUN

has improved _____. Today, _____-held

ADVERB   PART OF THE BODY

_____ are all the rage. In restaurants, you find many

PLURAL NOUN

_____ talking _____ into their _____ phones

PLURAL NOUN   ADVERB   ADJECTIVE

as they eat their _____. _____ percent of American

NOUN   NUMBER

_____ place their _____ calls from their

PLURAL NOUN   NOUN

cars as they are _____ to and from their home,

VERB ENDING IN "ING"

office, or _____. Walking and talking are now the "in"

NOUN

_____ to do. Over _____ percent of Americans walk our

NOUN   NUMBER

_____ streets with a hand-held _____ pressed

ADJECTIVE   PLURAL NOUN

against their _____.

PART OF THE BODY

MAD LIBS® is fun to play with friends, but you can also play it by yourself! To begin with, DO NOT look at the story on the page below. Fill in the blanks on this page with the words called for. Then, using the words you have selected, fill in the blank spaces in the story.

Now you've created your own hilarious MAD LIBS® game!

LOVE LETTER

ADJECTIVE _____

NOUN _____

NOUN _____

ADJECTIVE _____

ADJECTIVE _____

NOUN _____

NOUN _____

NOUN _____

PART OF THE BODY _____

NOUN _____

NOUN _____

NOUN _____

ADJECTIVE _____

VERB _____

NOUN _____

PLURAL NOUN _____

PART OF THE BODY _____

PART OF THE BODY _____

NOUN _____

VERB _____

NOUN _____

NOUN _____

PART OF THE BODY _____

VERB _____

PERSON IN ROOM _____

MAD◎LIBS®
LOVE LETTER

My _____ darling,
       ADJECTIVE

I love you more than _____ itself. Each minute away from
                              NOUN

you is a/an _____ , each hour a/an _____ eternity.
                NOUN   ADJECTIVE

Without you, life is dull, boring, and _____ . I feel like a
                                              ADJECTIVE

baby without my _____ , a toddler without my teddy
                          NOUN

_____ , a dog without its _____ . I can't get you out
     NOUN   NOUN

of my _____ . I can't stop thinking about the color of your
      PART OF THE BODY

_____ , the way you wear your _____ , the way you
    NOUN   NOUN

toss your _____ , your _____ laugh, the way you
                NOUN   ADJECTIVE

_____ a joke. This morning, when the mail _____
       VERB   NOUN

brought your special delivery _____ , my _____
                                PLURAL NOUN   PART OF THE BODY

skipped a beat, my _____ was in my throat, and my
                        PART OF THE BODY

_____ trembled so much, I could hardly _____ your
     NOUN   VERB

_____ . What you said set my _____ on fire. Do write
    NOUN   NOUN

again. Until then, I love you from the bottom of my _____ .
                                                        PART OF THE BODY

I will _____ you always,
              VERB

_____
            PERSON IN ROOM

This book is published by

PSS!
PRICE STERN SLOAN

whose other splendid titles include such literary classics as

The Original #1 Mad Libs®

Son of Mad Libs®

Sooper Dooper Mad Libs®

Monster Mad Libs®

Goofy Mad Libs®

Off-the-Wall Mad Libs®

Vacation Fun Mad Libs®

Camp Daze Mad Libs®

Christmas Fun Mad Libs®

Mad Libs® from Outer Space

Dinosaur Mad Libs®

Night of the Living Mad Libs®

Upside-Down Mad Libs®

Mad Libs® 40th Anniversary Deluxe Edition

Mad Mad Mad Mad Mad Libs®

Mad Libs® On the Road

Shrek Mad Libs®

Scooby Doo Halloween! Mad Libs®

Powerpuff Girl Mad Libs®

Scooby Doo Movie Mad Libs®

Austin Powers Mad Libs®

Worst-Case Scenario Mad Libs®

Scooby Doo Mystery Mad Libs®

Fear Factor Mad Libs®

and many, many more!

Mad Libs® are available wherever books are sold.